The Coming Day

a true Christmas story from China

Alice Burnett Poynor

Illustrations by Jean H. Berry

Copyright © 2011 Alice Burnett Poynor

All rights reserved. No part of this book may be used or reproduced by any means, graphic, electronic, or mechanical, including photocopying, recording, taping or by any information storage retrieval system without the written permission of the publisher except in the case of brief quotations embodied in critical articles and reviews.

WestBow Press books may be ordered through booksellers or by contacting:

WestBow Press
A Division of Thomas Nelson
1663 Liberty Drive
Bloomington, IN 47403
www.westbowpress.com
1-(866) 928-1240

Because of the dynamic nature of the Internet, any web addresses or links contained in this book may have changed since publication and may no longer be valid. The views expressed in this work are solely those of the author and do not necessarily reflect the views of the publisher, and the publisher hereby disclaims any responsibility for them.

Any people depicted in stock imagery provided by Thinkstock are models, and such images are being used for illustrative purposes only.

Certain stock imagery © Thinkstock.

ISBN: 978-1-4497-2002-5 (sc)

Library of Congress Control Number: 2011932549

Printed in the United States of America

WestBow Press rev. date: 07/05/2011

This Book Belongs To

_____

*I*t was very cold that winter. All over Northwest China, temperatures fell and snow lay on tree and hill and farm. Ice hung from eave and branch and temple roof.

In the town of Spring-of-Wine on the edge of the Gobi Desert a tiny girl awoke on the frozen mud floor in the corner where she slept. She threw off the sack covering her thin body and wobbled on cold-stiffened legs out into the street. She was not a pretty sight, this little creature, caked with mud and blood and the grime of the streets, huddled into herself for warmth.

For Gwa-gwa it was a winter like most others in her young life. A winter to be hungry, alone and very, very cold. When she was just a baby, Gwa-gwa's parents who lived up in the mountains of Mongolia had sold her to a rich woman in the town of Spring-of-Wine because they could not afford to look after her. But the rich woman who bought her did not love Gwa-gwa; in fact she was very cruel to her when she discovered that Gwa-gwa could neither hear nor speak. "She's no use to me," the woman said. "Bad enough that she's a girl, but a deaf-and-dumb one? What good is she? She'll just have to beg."

And so Gwa-gwa was turned out on the streets to beg all day. Every evening she took the few pennies she'd received back to her cruel owner. "Aah, you stupid, useless creature," the woman would yell, "Is that all you've brought me!" and she would take the hot poker from the fire and burn Gwa-gwa's legs and send her to bed with no supper. Each morning Gwa-gwa left home as soon as the sun was up and joined the other beggars on the street to survive any way she could. And Gwa-gwa, whose name means "Little Lonely" was indeed all alone.

Day after day Gwa-gwa dragged herself from house to house, shop to shop, holding out her hands for food. She used her knobby stick to beat away the packs of wild, angry dogs that snarled and snapped at her legs. She tapped her way along street after street, knocking on doors, standing on street corners and calling in her pitiful voice. She wailed and rubbed her stomach and pointed to her mouth. Everyone understood. After all she was not the only hungry, homeless child in China. Here and there a kind woman would put some steamed bread into her hands or a sympathetic man would let her eat some left-over noodles in his restaurant. But many days Gwa-gwa just went hungry.

One day as she turned the corner a street vendor was cooking dumplings. The smell of the warm bread sizzling in the oil was irresistible. He removed one from the deep frying pan and put it on the rack to cool. Mmm…Gwa-gwa could almost taste it already.

But just as she reached for it, a smaller beggar boy reached too. Immediately Gwa-gwa pushed his hand away and grabbed the dough. She shrieked and shook her stick in his face. Let him go somewhere else to beg! She shoved the food in her mouth and darted off, leaving him wailing.

As months went by, Gwa-gwa learned how to get food by begging or stealing. She learned how to use her stick to protect her from growling dogs or mean-looking people. But she never learned how to wash her clothes or comb her hair or eat politely. She never learned how to read or write or say what she wanted to say. Above all, she never learned how to be unselfish or truthful or patient. Gwa-gwa had no one to teach her. What was the use, after all, of teaching a girl – especially a girl that could neither hear nor speak?

And every day the woman who owned her grew more hateful till Gwa-gwa knew she could not go back to that wicked house. From now on she would sleep on the streets.

And then again came winter.

Every evening as snow fell and the sun went down, Gwa-gwa watched men and women bundle their thickly padded jackets around them and hurry home to their fires. It was then she shivered harder and searched for a corner, a staircase, a doorway, to shelter her from the bitter cold of a North China winter.

One December day just at sundown she trudged along Jade Street hoping for shelter. That's when she saw a sight that made her stop mid-shiver! A scraggly line of children snaked along the street toward a big, white tent that glowed with lamplight. As they marched, some banged on tins, others played wooden flutes or rang tiny bells or blew whistles. Gwa-gwa couldn't hear the sound of the strange band, but she sensed the excitement of the children and she followed them inside the tent.

They pushed their way to a spot on the floor, arguing and shoving for best position. Gwa-gwa pushed too. One boy spoke to Gwa-gwa and when she didn't answer, he laughed and the children around made fun of her, pulling at her ears and sticking out their tongues. But Gwa-gwa slapped away the hands and ignored them. After all, this place was warmer than outside so she sat firmly in her place and stared straight ahead. She had the feeling something was about to happen on the platform in front of her eyes.

In a minute a tall foreign lady with light colored hair appeared. As if her light yellow hair wasn't scary enough, on the end of her nose were bits of glass in a metal frame, perched there with nothing to hold them in place! How did they stay on? But never mind that – the lady was putting pictures on a strange fuzzy board. The picture showed a man reaching down over a rocky cliff to pick up a lamb that was caught in a bush. Gwa-gwa knew immediately what the picture was about: the sheep had wandered away and gotten into trouble and the good shepherd was rescuing him. The shepherds from the mountains nearby often carried lambs into Spring-of-Wine to sell in the marketplace. Everyone knew how the shepherds loved their sheep.

The other children around her in the tent seemed to be enjoying the story and Gwa-gwa sat very still, soaking up the warmth of the place, feeling the vibrations of song and laughter, and watching the smiles on faces. And every so often the light-haired foreign lady looked right into Gwa-gwa's face and smiled.

And then – all too soon – it was over. Out into the cold night they must go again. But this time, as Gwa-gwa was looking for a safe corner with a step to hide under, a Chinese lady in a brightly colored jacket touched her on the arm and spoke to her. Before she knew it, Gwa-gwa was with other children in a big dry building like a barn with mounds of straw on the floor. The icy wind couldn't reach them here; the snow would not cover her at night in here. The lady led her to a pile of fresh straw, and put Gwa-gwa's thin icy fingers around a tin bowl filled with steaming millet porridge.

Food. Real food. Warm food. Every swallow warmed her tiny cold body. And when that bowl was empty they refilled it! She gulped it down eagerly and rubbed her ragged sleeve across her mouth. Around the building other children were each being given a pile of straw and a bowl of food too. This was too good to be true! The straw prickled through her thin clothing and sometimes little insects crawled out, attracted by the warmth, but it was better than sleeping on the icy streets where she could be attacked by dogs or other beggars. Yes, this was much better. Warm and full, she made herself at home in her pile of straw and snuggled down to sleep.

The next night Gwa-gwa again went into the tent at sundown, following the children's band. The white tent glowed with the light of a lantern and the children's laughter and rhythm of music made it seem warm. Children with horns and drums played them and another foreign-looking lady led everyone in singing. Gwa-gwa could see from their faces all the others enjoyed the songs. Again the lady put pictures on a board as she talked and every so often, in the midst of talking, she looked at Gwa-gwa and smiled. And when she smiled, Gwa-gwa forgot she was called "Little Lonely".

Gwa-gwa went back to the tent night after night.

Then one night around Christmas time the tall lady was putting pictures on the board as usual when suddenly Gwa-gwa raised her shrill voice, pointed to the picture, and stammered. She didn't mind the other children's stares. She brushed off their attempts to keep her quiet. All that mattered was the picture! In the picture was a wooden barn with a feeding trough for animals. Many farms in the country had sheds with feeding troughs just like that for their cattle. That wasn't so unusual. But one thing in the picture made Gwa-gwa call out. In the cattle's feeding trough was a baby! And, like Gwa-gwa herself, the baby was sleeping on a pile of hay!

That night as Gwa-gwa returned to the shelter and burrowed down in her own straw bed, she thought of the picture she had seen. Who was this child who slept on the hay, just like herself?

Was he here in Spring-of-Wine?

Could she find him?

Did he sleep in one of the other shelters nearby?

Or was he all grown-up now?

She went to sleep with the questions.

Each day Gwa-gwa looked forward to nightfall when she would hurry to join the children in the big, white tent. And after the meeting, was the promise of the warm barn with a bed of clean straw every night and a bowl of hot cereal every day.

But it was too good to last.

One snowy day the woman in the pretty jacket who was in charge of the shelter took Gwa-gwa by the hand and led her out into the streets. The children who slept in the barn could not stay there forever. There were more people in Spring-of-Wine needing shelter; others must have a turn. Her bed of hay would be given to another child. Gwa-gwa felt an icicle of fear growing in her. Was she going to have to sleep on the street again? Or, worse yet, was the woman going to make Gwa-gwa go back to the cruel woman who owned her? What was happening?

Motioning for her to follow, the woman hurried through the lanes and alleys. Gwa-gwa tried to keep up. Finally the woman pounded on the door of a small mud-brick house. And when the door opened, there she was – the tall light-haired white woman with glasses on the end of her nose! The same lady that had told the stories in the tent!

The lady ushered them inside and Gwa-gwa felt the warmth of the fire in the stove and smelled the meat cooking for the next meal. After a few minutes' conversation, the Chinese woman in the colored jacket left. Now Gwa-gwa was alone with this strange looking woman with glass things to look through and long white hair. The lady's two friends, who looked just as odd, came out from another room to see what was happening.

The three of them turned her around and around, they touched the dog bites on her legs, they pulled apart the tangles in her matted hair, they talked and turned and poked and talked. And then they got to work.

Francesca had to wash Gwa-gwa's face and hands, yes, and her ears too. And Eva insisted on washing her hair, after cutting off all the tangles that were impossible to comb out. And Mildred took care of the sores on her legs and arms. They gathered up the rags she had been wearing and tossed them out. Then the lady with the glasses on her nose went into another room and came back with some clean clothes of her own which she wrapped around Gwa-gwa's thin, shaking body. And Liu, the cook, made her hot, steaming rice and crisp vegetables and spicy soup. Of course, the food came to the table in bowls and had to be eaten at the table from bowls with chopsticks and a spoon – no fingers! What funny people these women were.

But food was food and warm was warm, and clothes – even much-too-big-ones – were clothes. And the ladies DID smile.

Gwa-gwa didn't know it then but the lady and her two friends were missionaries who had come from England to China years before. Their names were Mildred and Eva and Francesca. They were getting ready to celebrate Christmas with special food and presents from their families in England.

But Gwa-gwa didn't know about Christmas; for Gwa-gwa it was enough to be warm.

"Gwa-gwa," said the missionary called Mildred, "Look at me." She turned Gwa-gwa's face toward her and made Gwa-gwa watch her lips. Mildred made lots of motions with her hands as she talked so Gwa-gwa got the idea even though she didn't hear the words.

"The shelter you have been sleeping in at night was opened by Christians in this city to help people just like you who had nowhere to sleep. They know how cold it is on the street at night. They keep piles of fresh straw there so each one can have a bed. But you cannot stay there forever, so they have brought you here. You never need to go begging around town again. You can stay with us."

And so on that Christmas Day for the first time in her life Gwa-gwa found a home. Always after that she called Christmas her "coming day" because it was the day she came to a real home.

And that meant some changes. Gwa-gwa was bright and quick to understand. She learned everything the missionaries taught her – how to eat neatly without dripping noodles all over her clothes, how to wash dishes when the meal was over, how to wash and comb her hair and, most of all, how to understand what people were saying and to make some sounds that others could understand. She rode in the cart with the missionary ladies when they went on long trips across the desert to take the Bible to other villages. She had a bed of her own and colored pictures to put up on her wall—even a picture of the good shepherd reaching down to pick up the lamb. And the warmth of Liu's cooking fire kept the chill off the air. That was a wonderful change!

Sometimes after supper the three women would take out a big folder of pictures. They put them on a big fuzzy board as they talked, and they let Gwa-gwa handle them too. She rubbed her finger gently along the lines of the drawings. The picture of a barn, a donkey, a star, and – here was that most wonderful picture of all – the baby asleep on the hay. What did it mean?

But Gwa-gwa couldn't ask.

Though she had a place to live, there was always loneliness in her that all the missionaries' kindness could not remove. Not able to hear or speak, Gwa-gwa was locked into her own silent world that no-one else could enter. She had no doubt she was loved by the missionaries but there were big lessons to learn.

One day when guests were coming, the cook baked some extra-delicious cakes and Gwa-gwa was allowed to put them on the table. She set them carefully in place beside the blue teapot with the little birds on it. This was a better-than-usual treat. She just had to have one!

Cautiously, she looked around to see that no one was watching. In a flash, her fingers reached out and scooped off one of the cakes. She put it in her apron pocket and walked quickly away.

But she had been seen.

"Gwa-gwa, where did the other cake go?" Mildred asked. "There were exactly eight on this plate—one for each of the guests. One is missing."

Gwa-gwa shook her head and shrugged her shoulders. Mildred persisted but Gwa-gwa refused to answer. Her face wrinkled in anger and she stamped off to her room.

"Gwa-gwa, listen to me!" Mildred said sternly. "If you want a cake you can certainly have one. You know you're welcome to anything we have to eat. But you must ask, not take it without asking. Even worse than that, you must not lie to us about it." Mildred carefully explained again and again and often she had to punish Gwa-gwa for misbehavior.

Living on the street had taught her to lie, and push other people away, and steal food. It was easy to see from their faces that the missionaries were displeased with such things – Gwa-gwa felt crushed when she saw their unhappy reaction. Yet there was no doubt that the missionaries loved her. Maybe she was like the little sheep who ran away from the shepherd and got in trouble. Was the shepherd unhappy with the little lamb? Yet clearly he loved him – wasn't he reaching over the cliff to pick him up? Silent questions tumbled around in Gwa-gwa's brain.

Finally, Christmas came again and this time Gwa-gwa was ready when the women pulled out the pictures of the barn and the donkey and the star. When at last they showed the picture of the baby on the straw, Gwa-gwa was able to ask what she had wanted to know for so long. Who was that baby who slept in straw just like herself?

Again Mildred gathered Gwa-gwa on her lap and turned her face toward her so Gwa-gwa could watch her lips and her hands.

"You know that you came to live with us on Christmas Day a year ago. That's your "coming day". That's Jesus "coming day" too. He came to earth at Christmas as a baby. He was born into a town where his parents had no home. Just like you, he had no room to sleep in the cold night. Just like you, he was given shelter in a barn, and put to bed in the hay.

But He was no ordinary baby. He was God, the God Who made all things. He owns all the camels in the Gobi desert and all the sheep on the hills; He had a beautiful home in Heaven much grander than the Temple of the Golden Sands or the governor's big home. He was King of all–he could have had a bed in a palace. He didn't need to sleep in a manger of hay.

But He came down to this earth to be like you – homeless and cold and poor – to show you how much he loved you."

Gwa-gwa shook her head and put her hands over her ears as if to say, "No. I have ears that can't hear and a tongue that can't speak. I am useless. The God-who-made-all-things does not care about ME."

"Yes, Gwa-gwa, YOU. Jesus does know you and He loved you even before you were born. He hears you, even when you can't say words; he talks to you deep inside you even though you can't hear His voice. We love you and made you part of our family here—God loves you even more and wants to make you part of His family."

Many times over many months the missionary had to repeat the story; Gwa-gwa knew Mildred and Eva and Francesca loved her; it was not so easy to understand that God loved her.

Christmas came and passed again. Little by little the snow of winter melted, the ice dripped away from the temple roof. Now the warming air didn't burn her nose when she breathed. Best of all, the warmer temperatures meant Mildred and Eva and Francesca could ride across the desert again to take the Bible to other villages and Gwa-gwa could go along! Here and there tiny purple desert flowers showed above the warming sands as they travelled from oasis to oasis. It was good to be warm. Good to feel the sun on her face as she rode on a donkey or walked beside the camels. It was good to feel loved!

Gradually, Gwa-gwa's heart began to warm too. She began to learn to talk to God with her heart and little by little she understood: just like the missionaries, God wasn't pleased with all the things she did, yet he loved her – just the way she was – and came to earth to show her that love. Her, Little Lonely!

As she grew older Gwa-gwa learned how to read and write and how to speak some words. When she grew older she went with the missionaries to their home in England. She loved to help tell Bible stories to visitors when they came. Very clearly she spoke the words so others could understand her. Very carefully she put all the pictures in the right place on the fuzzy board.

"I'm Gwa-gwa," she'd say. "I used to be 'Little Lonely' but I'm not lonely now. Christmas is my coming day—that's when I came to a home." Then she'd point to pictures of Jesus and say. "That's Jesus. Christmas is His coming day too." On the board she put the manger picture. "He left His beautiful home in Heaven and came to live on earth like a beggar just like me because He loved me." Then she would add the star and the shepherds. "And, can you believe it," she would say with a big smile, "even though He was the King of the world, He slept in the hay just like me!" and then she would add her favorite picture of all.

Epilogue

Gwa-gwa was a real little girl. This story is based on her life. Today the children of China may not sleep in barns and be cold and hungry, but one thing is still the same. Many of China's children have never heard of Jesus, who left Heaven for them, or of how He came to earth at Christmas. They have never heard because for many years parents were not allowed to teach them to believe in God or read them Bible stories. For many of them, even today, there is no church nearby where they can go.

As you read the story of Gwa-gwa and the baby in the straw this Christmas, will you take a minute to pray for the rest of China's children – and others all over the world, millions of them, who can never hear His story even though they have good ears? They will never ask "Who is Jesus?" because they have never heard of Him.

And pray for children (and their parents) the world over, like Gwa-gwa, who will never hear of God's love because of physical barriers. How can the message get to them? Whether barriers of ears and tongue or barriers of law, God can get His story into hearts. Pray that many people around the world would have a chance this year to hear for the first time the story of Jesus who came for them at Christmas.

Things to think about...

1. Can you find China on a map?

2. Do you know anyone who was born unable to hear or speak?

3. How do people who cannot hear or speak communicate?

4. Do you like Chinese food? Can you eat it with chopsticks?

5. Why did Gwa-gwa get excited about the picture of the baby?

6. Do you know anyone who has been to China? Maybe you can ask them about it.

A Closing Word to Parents

It was a very cold winter in Northwest China that day in the 1920s when a little girl who could neither hear nor speak was given shelter on a pile of hay in a barn. Gwa-gwa, whose name means "Little Lonely" came from the shelter to a permanent home with three British missionaries on Christmas Day, a day she afterward called her "coming" day. She is a real person; the missionaries who eventually adopted her are real, as are many of the details of the story. Gwa-gwa learned to know the Baby whose "coming day" was also Christmas and who, like herself slept in a bed of hay.

The story is adapted from the writings of the three British missionaries with the China Inland Mission who served in West China in the early 20th century. Their names are Mildred Cable, Eva French and her sister, Francesca French. They were often known as "The Trio". You will not find "Spring-of-Wine" on a modern map of China; that is the missionaries' translation of the Chinese name. Instead you can find the approximate setting on the edge of the Gobi Desert, in northern China and south of Mongolia. It was just a few miles beyond the Western end of the Great Wall. Its inhospitable climate, trackless miles of sand and steep mountain ranges meant few visitors ever attempted to enter this mysterious land – an area inhabited by Mongols, Turkestani, Tibetans and Uighur peoples and others, all unreached by the Gospel. It was a challenge the Trio could not ignore.

Besides their work in the province of Kansu, (or Gansu) they trekked many miles criss-crossing the Gobi Desert, traversing the Silk Road and going into Mongolia with the Gospel of salvation in Jesus Christ. For more of their ministry see the works referred to below. To learn more about the people of Asia and how the Gospel is reaching them today go to www.omf.org

The Gobi Desert. London, Hodder and Stoughton, 1942

The Challenge of Central Asia: a brief survey of Tibet and its border lands, Mongolia, Northwest Kansu, Chinese Turkistan and Russian Central. London, NY, World Dominion Press, 1929

Through Jade Gate and Central Asia: An Account of Journeys in Kansu, Turkestan and the Gobi Desert. London, Constable, 1927

A Desert Journal: Letters from Central Asia. London, Hodder and Stoughton, 1934

Also by Alice Burnett Poynor:

Silence, God Working: a study of the last five books of the Old Testament

From the Campus to the World

Spice Islands Mystery

East Into Yesterday

East of the Shifting Sands

East of the Misty Mountains

CPSIA information can be obtained
at www.ICGtesting.com
Printed in the USA
237146LV00001B